SET FREE

A BIBLICAL GUIDE TO DELIVERANCE
AND LASTING FREEDOM

SET FREE

A BIBLICAL GUIDE TO DELIVERANCE AND LASTING FREEDOM

TOM CORNELL

SOZO PUBLISHING

CONTENTS

DELIVERANCE IS A PART OF THE CHRISTIAN LIFE

A MISSING PIECE IN THE CHURCH TODAY

For many Christians, the topic of deliverance feels foreign, unnecessary, or even extreme. It's often associated with dramatic exorcisms, horror-movie-like manifestations, or something reserved for missionaries in distant lands. Some believers even question whether a Christian can need deliverance at all.

Yet, when we look at the ministry of Jesus, we find that deliverance was not a side issue—it was central to His mission.

"The Spirit of the Lord is upon Me, because He has anointed Me to preach the gospel to the poor; He has sent Me to heal the brokenhearted, to proclaim liberty to the captives and recovery of sight to the blind, to set at liberty those who are oppressed." (Luke 4:18 NKJV)

Jesus didn't just come to forgive sin—He came to set people free from bondage, oppression, and demonic influence. If deliverance was a core part of His ministry, why should it not be a core part of the Christian life today?

For too long, many believers have assumed that coming to Christ automatically eliminates all spiritual battles. But Scripture teaches that salvation is not the end of the war—it is the beginning. When we surrender to Jesus, we are enlisted in a spiritual battle where we must learn to recognize the enemy's tactics, resist him, and walk in the full freedom Christ provides.

This book is not about stirring up fear or creating an unhealthy obsession with demons. Instead, it is about exposing the ways the enemy operates and equipping believers with the biblical understanding, tools, and confidence to walk in total victory.

If you are a Christian, deliverance is for you—not just as a one-time event, but as an essential part of your walk with God.

What is Deliverance?

Before going further, let's define what deliverance actually means. Deliverance is the process of removing demonic influence and breaking spiritual strongholds that hinder a believer from walking in the fullness of Christ. It is the application of Jesus' victory over Satan, enabling believers to walk in freedom, authority, and wholeness.

Some Christians assume that deliverance is only for unbelievers. But the Bible teaches that demons are cast out, not off. If an unbeliever receives deliverance but does not fill their life with the Holy Spirit, righteousness, and the Word of God, they become vulnerable to even worse demonic attacks

(Matthew 12:43-45). This is why deliverance is primarily for believers—those who have been given the authority to resist the enemy and walk in freedom.

Just as healing is part of the Christian life, so is deliverance. No one would argue that a believer should never experience healing simply because Jesus has already paid for it. In the same way, even though Christ has won the victory over the enemy, we must apply that victory in our lives through repentance, renunciation, and resisting the enemy's schemes.

Deliverance is Not Just for the "Extreme" Cases

One of the biggest misconceptions about deliverance is that it's only for people who are experiencing extreme demonic oppression—manifesting demons, speaking with distorted voices, or losing control of their bodies. While these cases do exist, most of the enemy's work is subtle, hidden, and designed to go undetected.

Consider how Satan first deceived Eve. He didn't attack her with violence—he planted a deceptive thought that led her into agreement with his lies. That same tactic is still at work today.

Many believers struggle with:

- Persistent sins they can't seem to break free from
- Cycles of fear, anxiety, depression, or torment
- Addictions and destructive habits
- Constant feelings of rejection, unworthiness, or shame
- Unexplainable sicknesses or patterns of failure
- Family curses that seem to repeat across generations

These are all signs that deliverance may be needed. Yet, instead of recognizing the enemy's hand, many Christians assume these struggles are simply "part of life" or "just the way things are."

The truth is, if there is an area of persistent oppression, torment, or bondage in your life that doesn't align with the freedom Christ purchased for you, deliverance is likely needed.

The question is not "Do I have a demon?" but rather "Are there areas in my life where the enemy has gained access, and how do I close those doors?"

The Biblical Pattern of Deliverance

If deliverance is such an important part of the Christian life, why isn't it talked about more? One reason is that many churches have neglected or misunderstood this aspect of Jesus' ministry. But when we examine the New Testament, we see that deliverance was not an optional add-on—it was a normal part of the gospel message.

Jesus Commanded It

- *"And these signs will follow those who believe: In My name they will cast out demons…" (Mark 16:17 NKJV)*
- *"But if I cast out demons by the Spirit of God, surely the kingdom of God has come upon you." (Matthew 12:28 NKJV)*

Deliverance was a sign of God's kingdom advancing. Wherever Jesus went, He healed the sick, forgave sins, and cast out demons. These were not separate ministries—they were all part of restoring people to the fullness of God's design.

The Disciples Practiced It

- *"Then He called His twelve disciples together and gave them power and authority over all demons, and to cure diseases." (Luke 9:1 NKJV)*
- *"So they departed and went through the towns, preaching the gospel and healing everywhere." (Luke 9:6 NKJV)*

Jesus didn't just perform deliverance Himself—He trained His disciples to do it as well. Casting out demons was a normal part of Christian ministry from the very beginning.

The Early Church Continued It

- *"Philip went down to the city of Samaria and preached Christ to them… For unclean spirits, crying with a loud voice, came out of many who were possessed; and many who were paralyzed and lame were healed." (Acts 8:5-7 NKJV)*

The early church continued the work of deliverance as they spread the gospel. Wherever the gospel was preached, people were set free.

Why Every Believer Needs to Embrace Deliverance

If deliverance was such a central part of Jesus' ministry, why have so many believers ignored or rejected it today?

There are a few reasons:

- Lack of Teaching – Many churches avoid the topic altogether.
- Fear and Stigma – Some believe deliverance is "weird" or only for extreme cases.
- The Enemy's Deception – Satan works hard to convince people that deliverance isn't necessary.

But here's the reality: We are in a war whether we acknowledge it or not.

- *"For we do not wrestle against flesh and blood, but against principalities, against powers, against the rulers of the darkness of this age, against spiritual hosts of wickedness in the heavenly places." (Ephesians 6:12 NKJV)*

Many believers are struggling with battles that have a spiritual root but are trying to fix them with natural solutions. Deliverance is not the entire Christian life, but it is an essential part of it.

The goal of this book is not to make you obsessed with demons—it's to equip you to walk in complete freedom and victory in Christ.

What You Can Expect in This Book

Each chapter of this book will walk you through:

- The biblical foundation for deliverance
- How to identify areas where the enemy may have access
- How to remove legal rights and close open doors
- How to receive deliverance and break free from oppression

- How to walk in lasting victory and maintain your freedom

No matter where you are in your journey—whether skeptical, curious, or desperate for breakthrough—this book is for you. Deliverance is not a side doctrine or an optional experience. It is part of the Christian life. Jesus came to set captives free. That includes you. Are you ready to step into the freedom He purchased for you?

CHAPTER 1
DELIVERANCE IS THE CHILDREN'S BREAD
IS DELIVERANCE REALLY FOR CHRISTIANS?

Many sincere believers wrestle with the question, "Can a Christian need deliverance?" After all, if Jesus has set us free, why would we ever need to be delivered from anything?

Some assume that deliverance is only for unbelievers or those deeply involved in the occult, not for "regular" Christians who love Jesus, read their Bibles, and attend church. Others believe that once we are born again, demons have no access to our lives because we have the Holy Spirit.

However, when we look at Scripture, we find that deliverance was not only for outsiders—it was part of the normal life of the believer. Jesus didn't just come to save people from sin; He came to set them free from bondage.

"The Spirit of the Lord is upon Me, because He has anointed Me to preach the gospel to the poor; He has sent Me to heal the brokenhearted, to proclaim liberty to the captives and recovery of sight to the blind, to set at liberty those who are oppressed." (Luke 4:18 NKJV)

If Jesus came to proclaim liberty to the captives, then we must ask ourselves:

- Who are the captives?
- How do they get set free?

The truth is, many believers are living far below the freedom that Jesus purchased for them. They love God, yet still battle torment, addiction, cycles of failure, depression, and oppression. The issue isn't their salvation—the issue is that the enemy has found access into areas of their soul, and those areas need to be set free.

Deliverance is not just for the unbeliever—it is for the children of God.

Deliverance is the Children's Bread

One of the most compelling biblical proofs that deliverance is meant for believers comes from a short but powerful encounter between Jesus and a Gentile woman seeking deliverance for her daughter.

The Syrophoenician Woman's Request:

In Matthew 15:21-28, a Canaanite woman comes to Jesus and begs Him to cast a demon out of her daughter. At first, Jesus doesn't respond. When she keeps pressing Him, He makes a surprising statement:

"It is not good to take the children's bread and throw it to the little dogs." (Matthew 15:26)

At first glance, this might seem harsh. But Jesus is

revealing something important: deliverance is the children's bread.

In this statement:

- The children represent the people of God (at that time, Israel).
- The dogs represent those outside the covenant (the Gentiles).
- The bread represents deliverance—freedom from demonic oppression.

This woman, despite being a Gentile, responds with great faith, saying:

"Yes, Lord, yet even the little dogs eat the crumbs which fall from their masters' table." (Matthew 15:27 NKJV)

Jesus, moved by her faith, grants her request and delivers her daughter.

What Does This Mean for Us?

If deliverance was meant to be "the children's bread," then we must ask: Who are the children today? The answer is clear —those who have placed their faith in Jesus.

"For you are all sons of God through faith in Christ Jesus." (Galatians 3:26 NKJV)

If deliverance was reserved for God's people in the Old Testament and was later extended to those who entered by faith, then it follows that deliverance is now the inheritance of every believer in Christ. If you are in Christ, deliverance belongs to you.

Can a Christian Have a Demon?

One of the most common objections to deliverance ministry is the question, "Can a Christian have a demon?" The question itself is misleading. It assumes that demonic oppression is the same as possession, where a demon owns or completely controls a person. But biblically, the issue is not about ownership—it's about influence.

A Christian cannot be possessed by a demon because they belong to Christ. However, they can be oppressed, tormented, or influenced in areas of their soul and body.

The Temple as a Model for Deliverance

To understand this, we need to look at the biblical imagery of the Temple. In the Old Testament, the Temple had three parts:

- The Holy of Holies – Where God's presence dwelled (represents our spirit, which is born again and belongs to God).
- The Holy Place – The inner chamber where priests ministered (represents our soul—our mind, will, and emotions).
- The Outer Court – The place of sacrifice, open to the public (represents our body and flesh).

When Jesus cleansed the Temple (Matthew 21:12-13), He didn't cleanse the Holy of Holies—it was already pure. He cleansed the outer courts, because that's where corruption had entered.

In the same way, when we are saved, our spirit becomes the dwelling place of the Holy Spirit (1 Corinthians 6:19).

However, our soul (mind, emotions, will) and body can still be affected by sin, trauma, and demonic oppression.

This is why believers can still struggle with:

- Addictions
- Depression and anxiety
- Fear, torment, and irrational anger
- Cycles of sin they can't seem to break

These aren't just "bad habits" or "normal struggles"—in many cases, they are evidence of demonic oppression that needs to be broken through deliverance.

Why Would a Believer Need Deliverance?

Some Christians assume that once we are saved, all demonic influence automatically disappears. But salvation and deliverance are not the same thing.

Jesus raised Lazarus from the dead (salvation) but then told the people around him to "loose him and let him go" (deliverance) (John 11:44). Here's why believers may need deliverance:

1. Unrepented Sin – Sin opens the door to the enemy (Ephesians 4:27).
2. Generational Curses – Family patterns of sin and oppression can continue until broken (Exodus 20:5).
3. Trauma and Emotional Wounds – Past pain can create access points for spirits of fear, rejection, and torment.
4. Occult Involvement – Any participation in witchcraft, fortune-telling, or false religions can invite demonic influence (Leviticus 19:31).

Even though Jesus paid for our freedom, we must enforce it by closing these doors and casting out anything that does not belong.

Signs That a Believer May Need Deliverance

How do you know if you need deliverance? Here are some common signs:

- Persistent Struggles That Won't Break
- Addictions that seem impossible to overcome
- Uncontrollable anger, fear, or anxiety
- Suicidal thoughts or overwhelming depression

Spiritual Blockages

- A deep struggle to pray, read Scripture, or worship
- Feeling like a wall is blocking you from God
- Hearing internal accusations or lies that contradict God's truth

Unexplained Torment

- Sleep paralysis, nightmares, or sensing a dark presence
- Sudden mood swings that feel beyond your control

Patterns That Repeat in Families

- Generational cycles of addiction, poverty, or failure
- Patterns of broken relationships or divorce
- Chronic illness with no medical explanation

If any of these sound familiar, deliverance may be the missing piece in your breakthrough.

Freedom is Your Inheritance

Deliverance is not a side issue—it is an essential part of the Christian life. Jesus came not just to forgive sin, but to set captives free. The next chapter will explain how doors to the enemy are opened and how we can begin closing them. Are you ready to step into the freedom that belongs to you?

CHAPTER 2

HOW DO WE OPEN THE DOOR TO THE ENEMY? UNDERSTANDING LEGAL RIGHTS AND ACCESS POINTS

Many believers assume that because they have given their lives to Christ, they are automatically immune to demonic influence. They believe that since Jesus has won the victory, there's no way a demon could have any access to their life.

But if that were the case, why do so many Christians still struggle with torment, addiction, depression, irrational fears, or cycles of sin that seem impossible to break?

The truth is, while salvation gives us eternal life and restores our relationship with God, it does not automatically break every area of bondage in our souls and bodies. Even after we are saved, we must enforce the victory of Christ in our daily lives.

One of the primary ways Satan operates is by looking for open doors—legal access points that allow him to influence, oppress, or torment believers. Just like a thief can only enter through an unlocked door or window, demons need an entry point to gain access to a believer's life.

This chapter will explore how doors are opened to the enemy, how legal rights work in the spiritual realm, and how we can begin to close every access point through repentance, renunciation, and deliverance.

What Are Legal Rights?

The Bible shows us that the spiritual realm operates under legal principles. God is a just Judge, and even though Satan is a deceiver, he still understands how to work within spiritual laws to gain access to people's lives.

Consider these passages:

- *"Be angry, and do not sin: do not let the sun go down on your wrath, nor give place to the devil." (Ephesians 4:26-27 NKJV)*
- *"For whatever overcomes a person, to that he is enslaved." (2 Peter 2:19 NKJV)*
- *"Do you not know that to whom you present yourselves slaves to obey, you are that one's slaves whom you obey?" (Romans 6:16 NKJV)*

These verses reveal that:

1. Our choices can either yield to the Holy Spirit or give the enemy access.
2. Unrepented sin can create a foothold for demonic oppression.
3. Whoever we submit to spiritually, we give legal authority over us.

A legal right is any unresolved spiritual issue that allows demons to operate in a person's life. These legal rights must be broken before true deliverance can take place.

Common Open Doors to the Enemy

Unrepented Sin – The Most Common Access Point

Sin is the primary way demons gain access to a person's life. While believers are forgiven in Christ, ongoing, unrepented sin can create an open door for demonic oppression.

- *"He who sins is of the devil, for the devil has sinned from the beginning." (1 John 3:8 NKJV)*
- *"If we confess our sins, He is faithful and just to forgive us our sins and to cleanse us from all unrighteousness." (1 John 1:9 NKJV)*

Some examples of unrepented sin that can lead to demonic influence include:

- Sexual sin (pornography, adultery, fornication)
- Occult involvement (witchcraft, horoscopes, Ouija boards)
- Unforgiveness and bitterness (Matthew 18:34-35)
- Addictions (drugs, alcohol, gambling, destructive behaviors)
- Habitual lying, stealing, or deception

How to Close This Door:

1. Confess and renounce the sin.
2. Ask God for forgiveness.
3. Break any agreements with the enemy.

Prayer:

"Lord, I repent of (specific sin). I renounce every agreement I have made with the enemy through this sin. I ask You to forgive me and

*cleanse me from all unrighteousness. In Jesus' name, I close this
door to the enemy, and I command every demonic spirit associated
with this sin to leave me now!"*

Generational Curses and Family Patterns

Many believers struggle with issues that seem to run in
their families—generational cycles of addiction, poverty, sickness, or broken relationships.

- *"You shall not bow down to them nor serve them. For I,
  the Lord your God, am a jealous God, visiting the
  iniquity of the fathers upon the children to the third and
  fourth generations of those who hate Me." (Exodus 20:5
  NKJV)*
- *"Christ has redeemed us from the curse of the law,
  having become a curse for us." (Galatians 3:13 NKJV)*

These verses indicate that generational patterns can
persist until they are intentionally broken. Christ has made
provision for our freedom, but we must enforce it by
renouncing the sins of our ancestors and breaking every
inherited curse.

How to Close This Door:

1. Identify family patterns of sin, sickness, or failure.
2. Repent for any personal participation in these
   patterns.
3. Declare the finished work of Christ over your
   bloodline.

Prayer:

"In the name of Jesus, I break every generational curse over my life.

I repent for any sins of my ancestors that have given the enemy access to my family. I declare that through the blood of Jesus, I am set free from every curse. I renounce all agreements with generational bondage, and I command every spirit connected to it to leave me now!"

Trauma and Emotional Wounds

One of the most overlooked access points for the enemy is unhealed trauma. When we experience deep pain—whether from abuse, betrayal, or loss—it can create an open wound in our soul. If left unhealed, demons of fear, rejection, and bitterness can enter.

- *"The Lord is near to the brokenhearted and saves the crushed in spirit." (Psalm 34:18 NKJV)*
- *"He heals the brokenhearted and binds up their wounds." (Psalm 147:3 NKJV)*

How to Close This Door:

1. Invite Jesus into the painful memory and ask Him to heal you.
2. Forgive those who have hurt you.
3. Reject the lies of rejection and replace them with God's truth.
4. Occult Involvement and Cursed Objects

Any involvement in the occult—whether intentional or unintentional—opens the door to demonic oppression.

Examples include:

- Witchcraft, fortune telling, tarot cards, and Ouija boards

- New Age practices (crystals, energy healing, yoga with spiritual intent)
- Ancestral worship or secret societies
- Eastern religious practices (Buddhism, Hinduism, etc.)
- Owning cursed objects (idols, demonic artifacts, occult books)

Scripture says:

- *"Do not turn to mediums or seek out spiritists, for you will be defiled by them." (Leviticus 19:31 NIV)*
- *"And many who had believed came confessing and telling their deeds. Also, many of those who had practiced magic brought their books together and burned them in the sight of all." (Acts 19:18-19 NIV)*

How to Close This Door:

1. Renounce all past involvement in the occult.
2. Destroy any cursed objects in your possession.
3. Declare Jesus as Lord and ask Him to cleanse you.

Prayer:

"Lord, I renounce all involvement in (specific occult practice). I break every agreement I made with the kingdom of darkness. I declare that Jesus Christ is my only Lord, and I choose to follow Him alone. I destroy and remove every cursed object from my life. In Jesus' name, I close every door to the enemy and command every spirit associated with these practices to leave me now!"

Closing Every Open Door

The enemy can only operate where he has legal access. But

Jesus has given us the authority to shut every door and walk in complete freedom.

In the next chapter, we will go deeper into the process of deliverance—how to recognize when deliverance is needed, what happens in a deliverance session, and how to break free from the enemy's grip.

Are you ready to take the next step toward freedom?

CHAPTER 3

THE PROCESS OF DELIVERANCE – BREAKING FREE AND WALKING IN FREEDOM

Many people assume that deliverance is a one-time event—like flipping a switch, after which all their struggles disappear instantly. While deliverance can be dramatic and powerful, it is often a process rather than a single moment — deliverance is a process, not just an event.

Think of Israel's journey out of Egypt: they were freed from slavery in one night, yet they spent 40 years learning to walk in freedom. Likewise, deliverance involves:

1. Recognizing the areas of bondage
2. Repenting of any sin or agreements with the enemy
3. Renouncing and breaking every legal right the enemy has claimed
4. Casting out demonic spirits that have taken residence
5. Renewing the mind and filling yourself with the Holy Spirit

This chapter will walk through each step of the deliverance process, providing practical guidance on how to experience true freedom in Christ.

Recognizing When Deliverance is Needed

Before deliverance can happen, there must be a recognition that bondage exists. Many believers suffer for years because they don't realize that their struggles are spiritual in nature.

Signs That Deliverance is Needed

Spiritual Oppression:

- A strong resistance to prayer, worship, or reading the Bible
- A wall between you and God, even when you try to seek Him
- Hearing accusatory voices, condemning thoughts, or blasphemous thoughts you can't control
- A consistent heaviness, feeling spiritually numb or drained

Behavioral Patterns That Won't Break:

- Addictions (pornography, alcohol, drugs, gambling, food, etc.)
- Repeated cycles of anger, rage, or uncontrolled emotions
- Persistent fear, anxiety, or depression that does not respond to normal treatment
- Chronic suicidal thoughts or self-harm tendencies

Unexplainable Health Issues:

- Chronic illness that doctors cannot diagnose
- Constant fatigue or sudden unexplained pain during prayer or worship
- Unnatural sicknesses that seem to pass down through family lines

Disturbances in Sleep or the Home:

- Sleep paralysis or waking up feeling choked, suffocated, or pressed down
- Seeing dark shadows, demonic figures, or hearing voices at night
- Recurring nightmares of being attacked, chased, or tormented

If you find yourself identifying with any of these, deliverance may be needed. These are signs that the enemy has a foothold and needs to be cast out.

Preparing for Deliverance – The Power of Repentance and Renunciation

Clean House Before Casting Out the Enemy. Before demons can be removed, their legal rights must be broken. Repentance and renunciation are the two most important steps in preparing for deliverance.

- Repentance means turning away from sin and closing the door to the enemy.
- Renunciation means verbally canceling any agreements made with the kingdom of darkness.

Both are necessary before any spirits are commanded to leave.

Steps to Prepare for Deliverance:

1. Confess and Repent of All Known Sin

Prayer:

"Father, I confess that I have sinned against You in the areas of (list sins). I ask for Your forgiveness, and I turn away from these sins completely. I reject every lie of the enemy, and I receive Your truth."

2. Renounce Every Agreement with Darkness

Prayer:

"I renounce every agreement I have made with the enemy, knowingly or unknowingly. I break every tie to (list specific sins, practices, or curses). In Jesus' name, I cancel the enemy's legal right to my life."

3. Forgive Everyone Who Has Hurt You

- Unforgiveness is one of the biggest barriers to deliverance (Matthew 18:34-35).

Prayer:

"I choose to forgive (name). I release them into Your hands, Lord. I let go of all bitterness, anger, and resentment."

4. Remove Any Cursed Objects

- Get rid of occult books, idols, New Age objects, crystals, tarot cards, or anything connected to false religions.

Prayer:

"Lord, I remove every object that has given the enemy access to my life. I break every attachment to these things and dedicate my home to You."

Once these steps are complete, deliverance can begin.

The Deliverance Process – Casting Out Demons in Jesus' Name

Understand your authority. Deliverance is not about shouting, performing rituals, or struggling with demons for hours. It is about authority.

- *Jesus said, "In My name they will cast out demons" (Mark 16:17 NIV).*
- *The disciples returned to Jesus, saying, "Even the demons are subject to us in Your name!" (Luke 10:17 NIV).*
- *"Behold, I give you authority to trample on serpents and scorpions, and over all the power of the enemy, and nothing shall by any means hurt you." (Luke 10:19 NIV).*

Steps in a Deliverance Session

1. Invite the Holy Spirit to Take Control

- Begin with worship, inviting the presence of God into the session.
- Ask the Holy Spirit for discernment on what spirits are operating.

2. Identify the Demonic Spirit by Name (If Possible)

- Many times, spirits reveal their identity by the symptoms they cause (e.g., fear, lust, witchcraft, anger).
- Example prayer: "In the name of Jesus, I take authority over every unclean spirit in this person. Holy Spirit, reveal any hidden spirits that need to go."

3. Command the Demon to Leave

- Once legal rights have been broken, demons must obey the authority of Jesus.
- Example command: "In the name of Jesus Christ, I command every unclean spirit of (fear, lust, addiction, rejection, etc.) to leave now. You have no more legal right to stay. Get out now!"

4. Expect Physical Reactions

- Some people experience:
- Coughing, yawning, vomiting (as spirits leave).
- Feeling lighter, heat, or a strong peace as deliverance takes place.

5. Fill the Empty Space

- After a demon leaves, the person must be filled with the Holy Spirit (Luke 11:24-26).
- Example prayer: "Holy Spirit, I invite You to fill every part of me. I close every door to the enemy, and I dedicate my life fully to Jesus."

Maintaining Deliverance – Staying Free After Freedom

Deliverance is not the end of the journey—it is the beginning. After being set free, the believer must learn how to walk in freedom daily.

Keys to Staying Free:

- Daily time in God's Word (renewing the mind – Romans 12:2)
- Consistent prayer and fasting (staying spiritually strong)
- Surrounding yourself with godly community
- Worship and thanksgiving (keeping your spiritual atmosphere clean)
- Guarding your eye and ear gates (avoiding sinful influences)

Deliverance is Your Inheritance

The process of deliverance is not just for a select few—it is part of the normal Christian life. Jesus has already paid for our freedom; we must simply walk in it.

If you have gone through this process and experienced freedom, praise God! But remember, the enemy will always try to regain access. Stand firm, resist him, and continue to walk in victory.

Are you ready to fully step into the freedom Christ purchased for you? The next chapter will explore specific strategies for breaking generational curses, soul ties, and past agreements with darkness so that nothing remains that could pull you back into bondage.

CHAPTER 4

BREAKING GENERATIONAL CURSES, SOUL TIES, AND PAST AGREEMENTS WITH DARKNESS

FREEDOM MUST BE FULLY ENFORCED.

Many believers experience partial deliverance but later find themselves struggling with the same issues. They wonder, "Why do I still feel oppressed?" or "Why do these battles keep returning?"

The answer is often found in unbroken generational curses, ungodly soul ties, and past agreements with darkness. While demons can be cast out, if their legal rights are not fully removed, they may attempt to return.

Jesus warned: *"When an unclean spirit goes out of a man, he goes through dry places, seeking rest, and finds none. Then he says, 'I will return to my house from which I came.'" (Matthew 12:43-44 NKJV)*

To walk in lasting deliverance, every legal claim, attachment, or agreement with darkness must be broken. This chapter will guide you through the process of identifying, renouncing, and cutting off every hidden access point the enemy may have in your life.

Understanding Generational Curses

What is a Generational Curse? A generational curse is a repeated pattern of sin, sickness, or demonic oppression that runs through family bloodlines.

"You shall not bow down to them nor serve them. For I, the Lord your God, am a jealous God, visiting the iniquity of the fathers upon the children to the third and fourth generations of those who hate Me." (Exodus 20:5 NKJV)

This means that sins and demonic strongholds can pass down through families until they are broken. These are sometimes referred to as "bloodline curses" or "family patterns of bondage."

Signs of Generational Curses in a Family:

- Addictions: Alcoholism, drug abuse, gambling
- Cycles of Divorce or Broken Families
- Premature Death or Unexplained Sicknesses
- Poverty and Financial Struggles
- Mental Illness, Depression, or Suicide
- Occult Involvement Passed Down Through Generations

If you see a pattern of sin, sickness, or oppression in your family, it may be the result of a generational curse that needs to be broken.

How to Break a Generational Curse

1.Repent on behalf of your ancestors.

- Prayer: *"Father, I repent for the sins of my ancestors. I renounce every generational sin that has given the enemy access to my bloodline. I ask for Your forgiveness and cleansing."*

2.Break the curse in Jesus' name.

- Prayer: *"In the name of Jesus, I break every generational curse of (specific issue: addiction, sickness, etc.) in my family line. I declare that I am covered by the blood of Jesus, and the enemy no longer has legal right to my life."*

3.Declare Your New Identity in Christ.

- Prayer: *"I am a new creation in Christ (2 Corinthians 5:17 NKJV). I reject every generational pattern of sin, and I declare that I walk in the blessing of Abraham through Jesus Christ (Galatians 3:13-14 NKJV)."*

Understanding Soul Ties

What is a Soul Tie? A soul tie is a spiritual connection between two people that binds their souls together. Soul ties can be:

- Godly (Healthy Connections) – Marriage, godly friendships, discipleship
- Ungodly (Demonic Attachments) – Sexual sin, abusive relationships, manipulation

How Are Ungodly Soul Ties Formed?

1. Sexual Sin (1 Corinthians 6:16) – Sex outside of

marriage creates a spiritual bond that must be broken.
2. Toxic Relationships – Abusive, controlling, or manipulative people can create soul ties through emotional trauma.
3. Idolatry of a Person – If someone takes the place of God in your heart, a soul tie can form.

Signs of an Ungodly Soul Tie:

- You can't stop thinking about a person, even though the relationship was toxic.
- You feel spiritually drained or oppressed after being around them.
- You still feel emotionally bound to someone from the past, even if years have passed.

How to Break an Ungodly Soul Tie

1.Repent for any sexual sin or idolatry.

- Prayer: *"Father, I repent for any sexual sin, ungodly relationship, or emotional attachment that has formed a soul tie. I ask for Your forgiveness and cleansing."*

2.Renounce the soul tie in Jesus' name.

- Prayer: *"In the name of Jesus, I renounce every ungodly soul tie with (name). I break every connection, attachment, or hold they have on me. I declare that I am free."*

3.Destroy any physical items connected to the soul tie.

- Gifts, letters, pictures, jewelry—anything that holds an emotional or spiritual tie should be removed.

3. Renouncing Past Agreements with Darkness

The power of spoken agreements: Many people unknowingly make agreements with darkness through their words, actions, or beliefs.

- *"Death and life are in the power of the tongue."* *(Proverbs 18:21 NKJV)*

These agreements may have come from:

- Vows or Oaths – ("I'll never trust anyone again.")
- Curses Spoken Over Yourself – ("I'll always be broke.")
- Demonic Pacts – Secret societies, witchcraft, or occult practices

How to Renounce Past Agreements with Darkness

1. Identify any past vows, words, or occult involvement.
2. Renounce them out loud in the name of Jesus.
3. Ask God to replace every lie with His truth.

- Prayer: *"In the name of Jesus, I renounce every vow, agreement, or spoken curse I have made knowingly or unknowingly. I break every word curse over my life, and I reject every lie of the enemy. I declare that I am free and belong fully to Jesus Christ."*

Destroying Cursed Objects

Do Objects Carry Spiritual Influence? Yes! Certain objects can serve as spiritual anchors for demonic oppression.

"And many who had practiced magic brought their books together and burned them in the sight of all." (Acts 19:19 NKJV)

Examples of Cursed Objects:

- Occult books, tarot cards, Ouija boards
- Idols, statues, or objects used in false religions
- Jewelry, amulets, or charms tied to witchcraft

How to Remove Cursed Objects from Your Life

1. Ask the Holy Spirit to reveal any object that needs to go.
2. Destroy or burn these objects (don't donate them!).
3. Pray over your home and dedicate it to God.

- Prayer: *"Father, I consecrate my home to You. I remove every cursed object and anything that has given the enemy access. I declare that my home is covered by the blood of Jesus, and no weapon formed against me shall prosper!"*

Walking in Freedom

Breaking generational curses, soul ties, and past agreements with darkness is a vital step in lasting deliverance. However, deliverance is not just about getting free—it is about staying free.

Keys to Walking in Lasting Freedom:

- Daily time in the Word of God (John 8:32)

- A lifestyle of repentance and renewal (Romans 12:2)
- Surrounding yourself with strong believers
- Filling your life with the Holy Spirit (Ephesians 5:18)

The next chapter will focus on breaking free from addictions, strongholds, and destructive habits that keep people bound even after deliverance. Are you ready to step into full freedom? Let's continue the journey.

CHAPTER 5

FREEDOM FROM ADDICTIONS AND STRONGHOLDS

WHY DO SOME STRUGGLES PERSIST AFTER DELIVERANCE?

Many believers go through deliverance, experience a powerful breakthrough, and yet find themselves struggling with certain habits, addictions, or thought patterns long after the spirits have been cast out. They ask questions like:

- "Why am I still tempted?"
- "Why do I keep falling back into the same sin?"
- "Did deliverance even work?"

The truth is, deliverance removes the enemy, but it does not remove the patterns of the flesh.

Demons vs. The Flesh

- Demons must be cast out (Mark 16:17).
- The flesh must be crucified (Galatians 5:24).

Deliverance does not replace discipleship, self-discipline, and mind renewal. Even after a person has been set free from demonic bondage, strongholds remain—and unless they are broken, they will continue to pull a person back into captivity.

This chapter will help you understand strongholds, break free from addictions, and develop a lifestyle that ensures lasting victory.

1. What is a Stronghold?

A stronghold is a fortified place in the mind where the enemy has built a system of lies.

"For the weapons of our warfare are not carnal but mighty in God for pulling down strongholds, casting down arguments and every high thing that exalts itself against the knowledge of God, bringing every thought into captivity to the obedience of Christ." (2 Corinthians 10:4-5 NKJV)

Strongholds are ways of thinking that keep a person in bondage, even after demons have been removed.

Examples of Strongholds:

- Lust and Pornography – "I'll never be free from this."
- Fear and Anxiety – "Something bad is always going to happen."
- Poverty Mindset – "I'll always struggle financially."
- Rejection and Insecurity – "No one really loves me."
- Shame and Condemnation – "God will never fully forgive me."

Breaking free from strongholds requires a renewed mind and intentional action.

Addictions: The Flesh's Chains

How addictions work: An addiction is anything that controls a person and prevents them from living in freedom.

"All things are lawful for me, but I will not be brought under the power of any." (1 Corinthians 6:12 NIV)

Addictions enslave the mind, body, and emotions. While some addictions start as fleshly habits, many are reinforced by demonic spirits.

Common Addictions Among Christians:

- Pornography & Sexual Sin
- Alcohol & Drugs
- Gambling
- Overeating & Gluttony
- Video Games & Social Media
- Workaholism & Perfectionism

The Cycle of Addiction:

1. Trigger – Something triggers the craving (stress, boredom, loneliness).
2. Indulgence – The person gives in to the habit, feeling temporary relief.
3. Guilt – Immediately afterward, they feel shame and regret.
4. Vow to Change – They promise never to do it again, only to repeat the cycle.

To break this cycle, we must:

- Remove spiritual strongholds.

- Retrain the mind and body to crave righteousness.
- Build a system of accountability and discipline.

Breaking Free from Strongholds and Addictions

Step 1: Identify the Root Cause
Every addiction or stronghold has a root issue. Ask yourself:

- Why do I turn to this habit?
- What am I trying to escape?
- What lie do I believe that keeps me bound?

Often, addictions are tied to:

- Rejection – Using sin as a way to feel loved or accepted.
- Boredom – Filling empty time with sinful habits.
- Pain and Trauma – Using sin to numb wounds from the past.

Once the root issue is identified, it can be dealt with through prayer, healing, and mind renewal.

Step 2: Repent and Renounce the Addiction
Deliverance begins with repentance—turning away from sin and choosing obedience to God. Prayer of Repentance:

"Father, I repent for allowing this addiction to control me. I renounce every lie I have believed about this habit. I break every agreement I have made with darkness, and I choose to walk in freedom."

Once repentance has taken place, the demonic spirits behind the addiction must be cast out. Deliverance Command:

"In the name of Jesus, I command every unclean spirit connected to (name addiction) to leave me now. You have no more authority over my life. I am free in Jesus' name!"

Step 3: Renew Your Mind with the Word of God

Deliverance alone is not enough. If the mind is not renewed, a person will eventually fall back into the same habits.

"And do not be conformed to this world, but be transformed by the renewing of your mind." (Romans 12:2 NIV)

The enemy operates through deception. If you do not replace lies with truth, the stronghold will remain.

Replacing Lies with Truth:

- Lie: "I will never be free from this." → Truth: "Who the Son sets free is free indeed." (John 8:36 NIV)
- Lie: "This is just the way I am." → Truth: "I am a new creation in Christ." (2 Corinthians 5:17 NIV)
- Lie: "God is disappointed in me." → Truth: "There is no condemnation for those in Christ." (Romans 8:1 NIV)

Step 4: Remove Triggers and Temptations

One of the biggest mistakes people make after deliverance is keeping temptation nearby.

"Make no provision for the flesh, to fulfill its lusts." (Romans 13:14 NIV)

Examples of Practical Steps:

- Struggling with pornography? – Install an

accountability app, get rid of private access to the internet.
- Struggling with alcohol? – Remove it from your home, stay away from places that tempt you.
- Struggling with toxic relationships? – Cut off unhealthy connections.

If you don't remove the source of temptation, you are setting yourself up for failure.

Step 5: Develop Spiritual Disciplines to Stay Free
Deliverance happens in a moment, but freedom must be maintained daily.

Daily Prayer and Bible Reading – Strengthens your spirit and renews your mind.

- Fasting – Breaks the power of the flesh and increases spiritual authority.
- Accountability and Community – Helps keep you on track.
- Daily Worship and Thanksgiving – Fills your life with God's presence.

"Walk in the Spirit, and you shall not fulfill the lust of the flesh."
(Galatians 5:16 NKJV)

The more you feed your spirit, the weaker your flesh will become.

Your Freedom is Worth Fighting For

Breaking free from addictions and strongholds is not always easy, but it is 100% possible through Christ.

- You do not have to live in bondage.
- You are not too broken to be healed.
- You are not too weak to be set free.

Jesus paid for your freedom, but you must take action to enforce it.

In the next chapter, we will discuss how to walk in lasting victory over the enemy, including spiritual warfare strategies, resisting temptation, and keeping your spiritual atmosphere clean. Are you ready to not only get free—but stay free for life? Let's move forward into total victory.

CHAPTER 6
WALKING IN LASTING VICTORY OVER THE ENEMY
DELIVERANCE IS NOT THE END—IT'S THE BEGINNING

Many people go through deliverance and experience a powerful breakthrough, only to find themselves struggling again weeks or months later. They wonder:

- "Why am I still being tempted?"
- "Why do I feel attacked even after my deliverance?"
- "Did the demons come back?"

The truth is, deliverance is not a one-time event—it is the beginning of a lifestyle of freedom. Jesus taught that when an unclean spirit leaves a person, it may try to return:

"When an unclean spirit goes out of a man, he goes through dry places, seeking rest, and finds none. Then he says, 'I will return to my house from which I came.' And when he comes, he finds it empty, swept, and put in order. Then he goes and takes with him seven other spirits more wicked than himself, and they enter and dwell there; and the last state of that man is worse than the first."
(Matthew 12:43-45 NKJV)

This passage warns us that if we do not fill our lives with the things of God, the enemy will try to return. The key to maintaining deliverance is building spiritual strength, resisting the devil, and living a life fully surrendered to Jesus.

This chapter will teach you how to stand firm in your freedom and walk in lasting victory.

The Three Areas of Battle: The Flesh, The World, and The Devil

After deliverance, many people assume that all their struggles are over. But Scripture teaches that we still face three major enemies in our daily walk:

The Flesh– Our sinful nature that must be crucified daily.

"For the flesh lusts against the Spirit, and the Spirit against the flesh; and these are contrary to one another, so that you do not do the things that you wish." (Galatians 5:17 NKJV)

The World – A system designed to draw us away from God.

"Do not love the world or the things in the world. If anyone loves the world, the love of the Father is not in him." (1 John 2:15 NKJV)

The Devil – A personal enemy who actively seeks to destroy us.

"Be sober, be vigilant; because your adversary the devil walks about like a roaring lion, seeking whom he may devour." (1 Peter 5:8 NKJV)

To walk in lasting victory, we must learn how to fight against all three.

Resisting the Enemy: How to Shut Every Open Door

Deliverance removes demons, but if doors remain open, the enemy will try to return.

Common Open Doors That Must Be Shut:

- Sinful Habits – If you return to sin, you re-open the door to demonic influence (Ephesians 4:27).
- Negative Thinking – Strongholds remain if the mind is not renewed (Romans 12:2).
- Toxic Relationships – Being connected to ungodly people can pull you back into bondage (1 Corinthians 15:33).
- Unforgiveness and Bitterness – This can become a legal right for demonic torment (Matthew 18:34-35).
- Cursed Objects – Having occult books, idols, or unholy items in your home can invite demonic presence (Acts 19:19).

Practical Steps to Keep the Doors Shut:

1. Stay in the Word of God – Fill your mind with truth daily (Psalm 119:11).
2. Commit to Daily Prayer and Worship – Keep your spiritual life strong (1 Thessalonians 5:17).
3. Surround Yourself with Other Believers – Stay accountable (Hebrews 10:25).
4. Live a Holy Life – Guard what you watch, listen to, and entertain in your heart (2 Corinthians 7:1).
5. Declare Victory Daily – Use the authority of God's Word to cancel every attack (Luke 10:19).

Declaration:

"I am covered by the blood of Jesus. No weapon formed against me shall prosper. I resist the devil, and he must flee. I am a new creation in Christ, and I walk in total victory!"

The Armor of God: Your Spiritual Defense

One of the most important keys to staying free is putting on the Armor of God daily.

"Put on the whole armor of God, that you may be able to stand against the wiles of the devil." (Ephesians 6:11 NKJV*)*

The Full Armor of God (Ephesians 6:14-18):

1. Belt of Truth – Stay grounded in God's Word and reject the enemy's lies.
2. Breastplate of Righteousness – Live a life of holiness and purity.
3. Shoes of the Gospel of Peace – Stay firm in your faith and walk in the Spirit.
4. Shield of Faith – Use faith to extinguish Satan's attacks and doubts.
5. Helmet of Salvation – Protect your mind from deception.
6. Sword of the Spirit (Word of God) – Speak and declare Scripture against the enemy.
7. Prayer and Intercession – Stay connected to God daily.

Putting on the Armor of God is not symbolic—it is an intentional lifestyle.

Guarding Your Spiritual Atmosphere

Your environment affects your spiritual life.

Practical Ways to Maintain a Holy Atmosphere in Your Home:

- Remove unholy entertainment – Movies, music, and books that glorify sin can attract demonic influence.
- Fill your home with worship music and Scripture – Keep the presence of God strong.
- Pray over your home regularly – Anoint your home with oil and declare that it belongs to the Lord.
- Be careful of who you let into your space – Some people carry spiritual darkness with them.

If your home feels heavy, oppressive, or full of fear, it may be time to cleanse the atmosphere and invite the Holy Spirit to reign.

Prayer Over Your Home:

"Father, I dedicate this home to You. I remove every influence of darkness, and I invite Your presence to fill this place. Let peace, joy, and righteousness reign here. In Jesus' name, I break every assignment of the enemy over this home. Amen!"

The Power of Fasting in Spiritual Warfare

Some battles require more than just prayer—they require fasting.

"However, this kind does not go out except by prayer and fasting."
(Matthew 17:21 **NIV**)

Why Fasting is Important for Spiritual Strength:

- Fasting weakens the flesh and strengthens the spirit.
- Fasting helps break stubborn strongholds and addictions.
- Fasting increases spiritual sensitivity and authority.

If you feel that the enemy is attacking you, consider adding fasting to your routine.

Declaring Victory Over Every Attack

The enemy will always try to attack again, but you have authority over him. Use These Declarations Daily:

- "I am more than a conqueror through Christ!" (Romans 8:37)
- "No weapon formed against me shall prosper!" (Isaiah 54:17)
- "I take every thought captive to the obedience of Christ!" (2 Corinthians 10:5)
- "I submit to God, I resist the devil, and he must flee!" (James 4:7)

Speaking God's Word out loud is one of the most powerful ways to shut down every attack of the enemy.

Walking in Freedom Daily

Deliverance was never meant to be a one-time event—it is a daily walk with Jesus.

- You have been set free!
- You have the power to resist the enemy!
- You have authority through Jesus Christ!

As you continue in prayer, fasting, worship, and the Word of God, your spiritual strength will increase, and the enemy's power over your life will weaken.

In the next chapter, we will discuss how to help others experience deliverance, including how to discern spirits, lead deliverance sessions, and walk in your calling to set captives free. Are you ready to not only stay free—but help others get free too? Let's continue the journey!

CHAPTER 7
HELPING OTHERS EXPERIENCE DELIVERANCE
EVERY BELIEVER IS CALLED TO SET CAPTIVES FREE

Many Christians believe that deliverance is only for pastors, prophets, or those in "specialized" ministries. However, Jesus made it clear that deliverance is part of the life of every believer.

"And these signs will follow those who believe: In My name they will cast out demons…" (Mark 16:17 NKJV)

Deliverance is not just for church leaders—it is for anyone who believes in Jesus Christ. If you are a disciple of Christ, you have been given authority to help set others free.

This chapter will equip you with the wisdom, discernment, and confidence to minister deliverance effectively to others, whether it's in a formal setting or a casual conversation.

Understanding Your Authority in Christ

Before stepping into deliverance ministry, you must be fully convinced of one truth:

- Jesus has given you authority over the enemy.

"Behold, I give you authority to trample on serpents and scorpions, and over all the power of the enemy, and nothing shall by any means hurt you." (Luke 10:19 NKJV)

This means:

- You do not need to be afraid of demons.
- The enemy must obey when you command in Jesus' name.
- Deliverance is not about power struggles, but about legal authority—the kingdom of darkness must submit to the kingdom of God.

How to Recognize When Someone Needs Deliverance

Not everyone needs a full deliverance session, but many people carry demonic oppression without realizing it. Signs That Someone May Need Deliverance-
Spiritual Symptoms:

- Uncontrollable anger, rage, or hatred toward God or the church
- Hearing voices that tell them to harm themselves or others
- Extreme resistance to prayer, worship, or reading the Bible
- Blasphemous or tormenting thoughts that will not stop

Behavioral Symptoms:

- Addictions that seem impossible to break
- Sudden violent or destructive behavior

- Uncontrollable sexual perversion or lust
- Persistent depression, suicidal thoughts, or self-harm

Physical Symptoms During Prayer:

- Uncontrollable shaking, screaming, or manifestations
- Feeling choked, dizzy, or unable to breathe when prayed for
- Eyes rolling back or intense resistance to the name of Jesus

If these signs are present, it may indicate that a demon is influencing the person's life and deliverance is needed.

How to Conduct a Deliverance Session

Once you have determined that deliverance is needed, follow these steps:

Step 1: Create the Right Atmosphere

- Begin with worship and inviting the presence of God.
- Ask the Holy Spirit to reveal hidden strongholds or spirits.
- Have others praying with you, if possible.

Lead the Person in Repentance and Renunciation

Before casting out demons, legal rights must be broken. Lead the person in:

1. Repenting of all known sin

2. Renouncing generational curses
3. Forgiving anyone who has hurt them
4. Breaking soul ties and past occult involvement

Prayer:

"Father, I repent of every sin that has given the enemy access to my life. I renounce every agreement I have made with darkness. I break every generational curse and soul tie in Jesus' name. I forgive every person who has hurt me, and I reject every lie of the enemy. Holy Spirit, come and fill me with Your presence!"

Command the Spirits to Leave in Jesus' Name

After repentance, the demons must be cast out.

Command:

"In the name of Jesus Christ, I take authority over every unclean spirit tormenting this person. I command every spirit of (fear, lust, addiction, depression, etc.) to come out now! You have no more legal right to stay. Leave now in Jesus' name!"

What to Expect:

- The person may cough, yawn, vomit, or shake as spirits leave.
- Some spirits resist and argue—keep commanding with faith and authority.
- If the person is completely still and silent, ask them how they feel and continue praying as needed.

Fill the Person with the Holy Spirit

Deliverance is not complete until the person is filled with the Holy Spirit.

> *"And do not be drunk with wine, in which is dissipation; but be filled with the Spirit." (Ephesians 5:18* NKJV)

Prayer:

> *"Holy Spirit, I invite You to fill every part of this person's life. Fill them with Your power, Your peace, and Your presence. Let every place that was once occupied by darkness now be filled with Your light. In Jesus' name, amen!"*

How to Discern Different Types of Spirits

Not all demons operate the same way. Some are strongholds that need to be dismantled, while others are spirits that must be cast out directly. Common Spirits and How They Operate:

- Spirit of Fear – Causes anxiety, worry, panic attacks
- Spirit of Rejection – Makes people feel unloved, unworthy
- Spirit of Lust – Drives pornography addiction, perversion
- Spirit of Depression – Causes heaviness, suicidal thoughts
- Spirit of Witchcraft – Brings confusion, control, occult ties
- Spirit of Infirmity – Causes unexplained sickness, pain

The Holy Spirit will reveal what spirits are present if you ask for discernment (1 Corinthians 12:10).

What to Do If a Deliverance Seems Difficult

1. Make Sure Legal Rights Have Been Broken

If a demon refuses to leave, it may still have a legal right. Ask the person if there's any unconfessed sin, unforgiveness, or soul tie that hasn't been renounced.

2. Use Scripture Against the Enemy

Demons must obey the Word of God. *"Satan, it is written: 'Submit to God, resist the devil, and he will flee'* (James 4:7 NKJV). I command you to leave NOW!"

3. Fast and Pray If Necessary

Some spirits are stronger and require fasting in addition to prayer. *"However, this kind does not go out except by prayer and fasting."* (Matthew 17:21 NKJV)

4. Do Not Engage in Long Conversations with Demons

Jesus commanded demons to leave immediately—He did not have lengthy discussions with them. If a demon speaks, shut it down:
"You will be silent in Jesus' name!"

How to Help Someone Maintain Their Deliverance

Deliverance is not complete until the person is equipped to stay free. Keys to Maintaining Deliverance:

- Daily Bible Reading – Fills the mind with truth (Romans 12:2).

- Regular Prayer and Worship – Strengthens the spirit (Ephesians 6:18).
- Surrounding Themselves with Other Believers – Provides accountability (Hebrews 10:25).
- Breaking Old Habits and Removing Triggers – Keeps doors closed to the enemy (Romans 13:14).
- Speaking Victory Daily – Declares their authority in Christ (Luke 10:19).

You Were Made for This!

Deliverance is not a ministry for the "elite"—it is a ministry for every believer.

- You have authority.
- You are anointed.
- You can set captives free!

Jesus is still delivering people today, and He wants to use you to bring freedom to others.

In the next chapter, we will explore how to bring deliverance into the local church, how to disciple people after deliverance, and how to create a culture of freedom within your community.

Are you ready to help others walk in the freedom that Christ has purchased for them? Let's continue the journey!

CHAPTER 8
ESTABLISHING A CULTURE OF DELIVERANCE IN THE CHURCH
DELIVERANCE IS FOR THE WHOLE CHURCH

For many churches, deliverance is either ignored completely or treated as a side ministry for a select few. However, when we look at the early church, we see that deliverance was a normal part of the gospel message.

- *"And they cast out many demons, and anointed with oil many who were sick, and healed them." (Mark 6:13 NKJV)*
- *"For unclean spirits, crying with a loud voice, came out of many who were possessed; and many who were paralyzed and lame were healed." (Acts 8:7 NKJV)*

The apostles and early church leaders knew that preaching the gospel and casting out demons went hand in hand. But today, many churches are uncomfortable with the topic of deliverance because:

- They fear controversy or excess.
- They lack understanding or training.
- They are influenced by a Western mindset that ignores the supernatural.

However, we cannot afford to ignore deliverance. If we want to see the full power of the gospel, we must bring deliverance back into the church as a normal part of ministry.

This chapter will show you how to:

- Establish a healthy and biblical culture of deliverance.
- Train leaders and members to walk in spiritual authority.
- Ensure that deliverance is done in wisdom, order, and under proper covering.

Why the Church Needs Deliverance Ministry

Many believers love Jesus but still struggle. They pray, read their Bible, and attend church, yet they:

- Feel stuck in cycles of sin and addiction.
- Experience unexplainable fear, depression, or torment.
- Deal with generational bondage and patterns of failure.

This is not normal Christianity—it is oppression that must be broken. Jesus did not only preach about salvation—He demonstrated the kingdom by setting people free.

"The Spirit of the Lord is upon Me, because He has anointed Me to preach the gospel to the poor; He has sent Me to heal the brokenhearted, to proclaim liberty to the captives and recovery of sight to the blind, to set at liberty those who are oppressed." (Luke 4:18 NKJV)

The modern church must embrace all aspects of Jesus'

ministry, not just preaching and teaching, but also healing and deliverance.

How to Build a Healthy Deliverance Culture

1. Teach Biblical Deliverance Regularly. Many Christians fear deliverance because they have never been properly taught about it. The first step in building a deliverance culture is teaching what the Bible says.

- Preach on the authority of the believer (Luke 10:19).
- Explain how demons gain access (Ephesians 4:27).
- Teach on how Jesus and the apostles cast out demons (Mark 16:17, Acts 8:7).
- Address common misconceptions about deliverance (e.g., "Christians can't have demons").

When believers understand deliverance, they will stop fearing it and start walking in it.

2. Equip and train leaders for deliverance ministry. Deliverance should not be limited to one person or a select few—it should be a trained ministry within the church.

How to Train a Deliverance Team:

1. Select spiritually mature leaders who walk in holiness and biblical authority.
2. Train them in discernment and spiritual warfare (1 Corinthians 12:10).
3. Teach them how to conduct deliverance sessions in wisdom and order.
4. Ensure they remain accountable to church leadership.

5. Require personal integrity and prayer life—
deliverance ministers must be spiritually strong.

A healthy deliverance team will prevent unnecessary chaos and disorder.

3. Create a safe and orderly environment for deliverance. Many churches avoid deliverance because they fear chaotic manifestations. However, deliverance does not have to be disorderly.

"For God is not the author of confusion but of peace, as in all the churches of the saints." (1 Corinthians 14:33 NKJV)

- Deliverance should be done in an orderly setting.
- Have trained ministers available to assist.
- Do not allow sensationalism or showmanship— deliverance is about setting people free, not entertainment.
- Encourage privacy for personal deliverance (not everyone needs to manifest publicly).

The goal is to make deliverance safe, accessible, and normal for everyone.

When and How to Incorporate Deliverance in Church Services

Deliverance can take place in different settings depending on the need.

During Altar Ministry in Regular Services

- Many churches offer prayer after the sermon—this is an opportunity for deliverance to take place.

- If someone manifests, trained leaders should take them aside for private deliverance.

Special Deliverance Services or Nights

- Some churches designate a specific time for deliverance-focused ministry.
- This allows people to come with expectation, knowing that freedom is available.

Small Groups and Personal Sessions

- Some deliverance is best done in a private setting where people can confess and receive personal ministry.
- Leaders should be available to meet with individuals who need deeper freedom.

Protecting the Church from False Deliverance and Abuses

Discernment is essential. Not every manifestation is a demon. Some are:

- Emotional responses (people reacting to conviction).
- Psychological struggles (not every issue is spiritual).

How to Discern True Deliverance Needs:

- Look for biblical signs of demonic oppression (e.g., unnatural resistance to prayer, hearing voices, violent manifestations).
- Ask the Holy Spirit for wisdom and discernment (1 Corinthians 12:10).

- If in doubt, do not force deliverance—God will reveal when it is truly needed.

Avoiding Manipulation and Control in Deliverance Ministry
Some deliverance ministries fall into error by:

- Making people dependent on them instead of teaching believers to stand firm.
- Charging money for deliverance (this is unbiblical!).
- Encouraging extreme manifestations as proof of deliverance.

True deliverance:

- Empowers believers to maintain their freedom through the Word.
- Keeps Christ at the center, not the minister.
- Operates in humility and love, not pride and manipulation.

What Happens After Deliverance? How to Disciple People into Lasting Freedom

Deliverance is not just about casting out demons—it's about making disciples who live in freedom.

"Go therefore and make disciples of all nations." (Matthew 28:19 NKJV)

To prevent people from falling back into bondage, they need:

- Biblical teaching – How to resist the enemy and walk in victory (James 4:7).

- Accountability and community – Freedom is maintained in a strong faith environment (Hebrews 10:25).
- Prayer and fasting – Keeping the flesh under control (Matthew 17:21).
- A daily lifestyle of holiness – Walking in obedience to God's Word (Ephesians 4:27).

Every deliverance session should include guidance on how to stay free.

Bringing Deliverance Back to the Church

The modern church must return to the power of the early church.

- Deliverance must be preached.
- Deliverance must be practiced.
- Deliverance must be made normal again.

Jesus said:"If the Son makes you free, you shall be free indeed."
(John 8:36 NKJV)

The next chapter will discuss testimonies of deliverance, real-life freedom stories, and how to activate your faith to walk in this power daily.

Are you ready to see your church become a place of true freedom and transformation? Let's continue the journey!

CHAPTER 9

TESTIMONIES OF FREEDOM AND ACTIVATING YOUR FAITH FOR DELIVERANCE

THE POWER OF TESTIMONIES

O ne of the most powerful ways to build faith for deliverance is through testimonies.

"And they overcame him by the blood of the Lamb and by the word of their testimony." (Revelation 12:11 NKJV)

When we hear how others have been set free, it strengthens our faith that God can do the same for us. This chapter will highlight real-life stories of deliverance, provide biblical examples of freedom, and teach you how to activate your faith to walk in power.

Biblical Testimonies of Deliverance

Throughout the Bible, we see Jesus setting captives free. We see that with the Demonized Man in the Synagogue (Mark 1:23-27)

- A man inside a synagogue (a place of worship) had an unclean spirit.

- The demon cried out when Jesus spoke with authority.
- Jesus commanded the spirit to leave, and the man was instantly free.

Key Lesson:
Even religious people can need deliverance. Demons hide well in religious environments but cannot withstand the authority of Christ.

The Woman Bent Over by a Spirit of Infirmity (Luke 13:10-13)

- A woman had been crippled for 18 years by a demonic spirit.
- Jesus declared her free and laid hands on her.
- Immediately, she stood up straight and was healed.

Key Lesson:
Not all sickness is just physical—some are spiritual in nature. Deliverance can bring healing where medical treatment has failed.

The Gerasene Demoniac (Mark 5:1-20)

- A man tormented by demons lived in a graveyard, cutting himself.
- When Jesus approached, the demons begged to be cast into pigs.
- After deliverance, the man was completely transformed.

Key Lesson:
Some extreme behaviors, such as self-harm, suicidal tendencies, or uncontrollable rage, may be demonic in nature. Jesus has total authority to bring restoration.

Modern-Day Testimonies of Deliverance

Freedom from Pornography and Lust

- A young man struggled with pornography addiction for over a decade.
- Despite prayer and fasting, the cycle of sin continued.
- Through deliverance, a spirit of lust was cast out.
- Afterward, the addiction was completely broken, and his mind was restored.

Key Lesson:
Some addictions are not just habits—they are spiritual strongholds that require deliverance.

Deliverance from Night Terrors and Sleep Paralysis

- A woman suffered from demonic attacks in her sleep for years.
- She would wake up paralyzed, seeing dark figures in her room.
- After breaking ties with occult practices from her past, she was delivered.
- Since then, she has slept peacefully every night.

Key Lesson:
The enemy often attacks in the night. Removing cursed objects, renouncing occult involvement, and praying over your home can break these attacks.

Breaking Generational Curses of Poverty

- A man noticed a pattern of financial struggle in his family.

- No matter how hard he worked, money would disappear unexpectedly.
- Through prayer, he discovered a generational curse of poverty.
- He renounced the curse, broke agreements with past financial failures, and began walking in biblical financial principles.
- Within months, he experienced supernatural provision and financial breakthroughs.

Key Lesson:
Some financial struggles are not just bad decisions—they are spiritual. Breaking generational curses can unlock financial freedom.

How to Activate Your Faith for Deliverance

Many people struggle with doubt when it comes to deliverance. They think:

- "What if it doesn't work?"
- "Maybe my case is different."
- "I've tried before and nothing happened."

But deliverance requires faith. Jesus told people:

"According to your faith let it be to you." (Matthew 9:29 NKJV)

If you want to experience complete freedom, you must:
A. Believe That Deliverance is For You
Many people think deliverance is for "other people" but not for them. That is a lie.

- Jesus came to set YOU free! (Luke 4:18)

- God has not called you to a life of bondage!
  (Romans 8:15)
- Deliverance is the children's bread! (Matthew 15:26)

Faith Declaration:

"I believe that Jesus has already won my victory! I receive my
deliverance today in Jesus' name!"

B. Renounce Every Agreement with the Enemy

Many believers unknowingly agree with the enemy's lies.
To walk in freedom, you must break these agreements.

Example Renunciation Prayer:

*"In Jesus' name, I renounce every lie of the enemy that says I cannot
be free. I break every agreement I have made with fear, addiction,
lust, or failure. I cancel the enemy's plans, and I declare that I
belong fully to Jesus Christ!"*

C. Walk in Obedience and Holiness

Deliverance removes demonic oppression, but obedience
keeps you free.

*"Submit to God. Resist the devil, and he will flee from you." (James
4:7 NIV)*

Practical Steps to Stay Free:

- Avoid places, people, and habits that lead back
  into sin.
- Fast and pray regularly to keep your spirit strong.

- Surround yourself with godly believers who encourage you.
- Fill your home with worship, prayer, and the Word of God.

Faith Declaration:

"I will walk in the freedom that Christ has given me! I will resist the devil and live a holy life in Jesus' name!"

Helping Others Activate Their Faith for Deliverance

After you have been set free, God wants to use you to help others.

A. Be Bold in Sharing Your Testimony

Your testimony has power! When you share what Jesus has done for you:

- It strengthens your own faith.
- It encourages others to believe for their freedom.
- It glorifies God and exposes the devil's defeat.

Challenge:
Share your deliverance story with at least one person this week.

B. Pray for Others to Receive Freedom

Once you have experienced deliverance, you can pray for others to be set free.

"Freely you have received, freely give." (Matthew 10:8 NKJV)

If someone is struggling, offer to pray with them.

Prayer for Someone Needing Deliverance:

"Father, I thank You for Your power to set captives free. Right now, in Jesus' name, I command every spirit of fear, addiction, and torment to leave this person. I declare that they are free in the name of Jesus!"

Your Freedom is Just the Beginning

Your deliverance is not the end—it is the beginning of a powerful journey with God.

- You have been set free!
- You have authority over the enemy!
- You are called to help others experience freedom!

What's Next?

- Continue growing in faith through prayer, fasting, and the Word.
- Testify of your deliverance and encourage others.
- Step into your calling to help set captives free.

Jesus said:

"If the Son makes you free, you shall be free indeed." (John 8:36 NKJV)

Are you ready to live a life of total freedom and victory? The journey is just beginning!

CHAPTER 10

WALKING IN LIFELONG FREEDOM AND LEADING OTHERS TO DELIVERANCE

FREEDOM IS A JOURNEY, NOT JUST AN EVENT

Many people believe that once they receive deliverance, the battle is over—but the truth is, deliverance is just the beginning of a life-long journey of walking in freedom, authority, and holiness.

"Stand fast therefore in the liberty by which Christ has made us free, and do not be entangled again with a yoke of bondage."
(Galatians 5:1 NKJV)

Deliverance removes demonic influence, but it is our responsibility to remain free by developing spiritual disciplines and growing in our walk with God.

This final chapter will equip you to:

- Walk in consistent victory over the enemy.
- Strengthen your spiritual life so that you do not fall back into bondage.
- Disciple others so they too can experience lasting deliverance.

The Five Keys to Lifelong Freedom

The enemy is always looking for a way back in (Matthew 12:43-45). To stay free, you must be intentional about maintaining your spiritual health.

Key #1: Live a Lifestyle of Prayer
Prayer is the greatest weapon in spiritual warfare. If you stop praying, you will become spiritually weak and vulnerable to attack.

- *"Pray without ceasing."* (1 Thessalonians 5:17 NKJV)
- *"Watch and pray, lest you enter into temptation."* (Matthew 26:41 NKJV)

Action Step:

- Set a daily prayer schedule and stick to it.
- Spend time in worship, thanksgiving, and intercession.

Key #2: Guard Your Mind and Thoughts
The biggest battlefield is the mind—the enemy attacks through thoughts, lies, and temptations.

- *"Be transformed by the renewing of your mind."* (Romans 12:2 NKJV)
- *"Take every thought captive to the obedience of Christ."* (2 Corinthians 10:5 NKJV)

Action Step:

- Reject negative and demonic thoughts—replace them with truth from God's Word.
- Speak faith-filled declarations over yourself daily.

Key #3: Walk in Holiness and Purity

Sin opens the door to the enemy. To stay free, you must commit to a life of obedience and holiness.

- *"Pursue peace with all people, and holiness, without which no one will see the Lord." (Hebrews 12:14 NKJV)*
- *"Make no provision for the flesh, to fulfill its lusts." (Romans 13:14 NKJV)*

Action Step:

- Identify any areas of compromise and remove them from your life.
- Be accountable to mature believers who will help you stay strong.

Key #4: Surround Yourself with the Right People

You cannot stay free alone—you need a strong Christian community.

- *"Do not be deceived: 'Evil company corrupts good habits.'" (1 Corinthians 15:33 NKJV)*
- *"He who walks with wise men will be wise, but the companion of fools will be destroyed." (Proverbs 13:20 NKJV)*

Action Step:

- Be part of a Bible-believing church that embraces deliverance and discipleship.
- Cut off toxic relationships that pull you back into sin.

Key #5: Stay Filled with the Holy Spirit

Deliverance is not just about casting demons out—it's about being filled with the Spirit so there is no room for the enemy to return.

- *"Be filled with the Spirit." (Ephesians 5:18* NKJV)
- *"Walk in the Spirit, and you shall not fulfill the lust of the flesh." (Galatians 5:16* NKJV)

Action Step:

- Spend time praying in the Spirit daily.
- Develop a strong relationship with the Holy Spirit.

Helping Others Stay Free: Discipleship After Deliverance

Jesus never just cast out demons and left people alone—He always called them into a lifestyle of following Him.

- *"Go therefore and make disciples of all nations." (Matthew 28:19* NKJV)

To truly help others walk in lasting freedom, they need discipleship and mentorship.

How to Disciple Someone After Deliverance:

- Teach them how to pray and read the Bible daily.
- Encourage them to stay accountable to strong believers.
- Help them recognize and reject the enemy's lies.
- Walk with them through struggles and encourage them.

Avoiding the Pitfalls of Deliverance Ministry

While deliverance is powerful and necessary, some people fall into common traps that can lead to error.

A. Deliverance Without Discipleship

- Some people seek constant deliverance sessions without making an effort to grow spiritually.
- Deliverance is not a substitute for renewing the mind and walking in obedience.

Solution: Always combine deliverance with solid biblical teaching and discipleship.

B. Overemphasizing Demons Instead of Jesus

- Some people become obsessed with deliverance and start blaming every problem on a demon.
- The focus of the Christian life is Jesus—not demons.

Solution: Make sure you are growing in Christ and not just focusing on demons.

C. False Teachings and Sensationalism

- Some people exaggerate manifestations and turn deliverance into a show.
- Others promote unbiblical teachings, such as charging money for deliverance (which is completely wrong!).

Solution: Stay biblically grounded and avoid excesses.

What to Do If You Feel Attacked Again

Even after deliverance, the enemy may try to attack again. If this happens:

- Do not panic! Attacks are normal, but they do not mean your deliverance failed.
- Resist the devil in prayer (James 4:7).
- Declare the Word of God out loud.
- Check for any open doors and close them immediately.
- Seek prayer and agreement with other believers.

Stepping into Your Calling to Set Captives Free

Once you have experienced freedom, God wants to use you to help others. Jesus said:

"The Spirit of the Lord is upon Me, because He has anointed Me to preach the gospel to the poor; He has sent Me to heal the brokenhearted, to proclaim liberty to the captives…" (Luke 4:18 NKJV)

This means that setting people free is part of the gospel!

Ways to Step into Deliverance Ministry:

- Start by praying for people in your church or community.
- Teach others about deliverance and spiritual warfare.
- Be available to minister deliverance when needed.
- Continue learning and growing in wisdom and discernment.

You do not need to be a pastor or leader—if you are a believer in Jesus Christ, you have authority over the enemy.

A Life of Victory and Freedom

Deliverance is not just an event—it is a lifestyle of:

- Spiritual discipline
- Obedience to God
- Daily surrender to the Holy Spirit

Final Encouragement:

- You are free, and you are called to set others free.
- You have authority over the enemy through Christ.
- God has anointed you to walk in lifelong victory.

Jesus said:

"Behold, I give you authority… over all the power of the enemy, and nothing shall by any means hurt you." (Luke 10:19 NKJV)

This is your time to rise up and walk in the full freedom and power that Christ has given you.

Final Challenge:

- Will you commit to walking in freedom daily?
- Will you help others experience the same deliverance you have received?
- Will you step into your calling to set captives free?

The journey is just beginning. Go forward in power, authority, and total victory in Christ!

APPENDIX: PRACTICAL TOOLS FOR DELIVERANCE AND SPIRITUAL WARFARE

This section provides essential prayers, scriptures, and practical guidance to help you maintain deliverance, resist the enemy, and set others free. Use this as a quick reference guide whenever you need spiritual breakthrough.

Prayers for Deliverance & Freedom

These prayers can be used for self-deliverance or to lead someone through a deliverance session.

A. Prayer of Repentance
(Breaking Legal Rights of the Enemy)

"Heavenly Father, I come before You in the name of Jesus Christ. I repent for every sin, known and unknown, that has given the enemy access to my life. I ask for Your forgiveness and cleansing through the blood of Jesus. I turn away from all darkness and choose to walk in righteousness. Thank You for Your mercy and grace. In Jesus' name, amen."

B. Prayer to Renounce Generational Curses

"In the name of Jesus, I renounce every generational curse, sin, and iniquity that has passed down my bloodline. I declare that I am a new creation in Christ. Every generational spirit operating in my family, I command you to leave now in Jesus' name! I break every cycle of addiction, poverty, sickness, and failure. I declare that the blood of Jesus has set me free!"

C. Prayer to Break Soul Ties

"Father, in the name of Jesus, I break every ungodly soul tie with (name the person or people)*. I renounce all emotional, sexual, and spiritual connections that have kept me bound. I cancel every agreement I made with them, knowingly or unknowingly. I declare that I am free, and my soul belongs fully to You. Every spirit connected to these ties must leave now, in Jesus' name!"*

D. Prayer for Deliverance from Demonic Oppression

"In the name of Jesus Christ, I take authority over every unclean spirit tormenting my life. I command every spirit of fear, anxiety, depression, addiction, lust, and witchcraft to leave me now! You have no legal right to stay. I am covered by the blood of Jesus, and I reject every lie of the enemy. Holy Spirit, fill me completely and take full control of my life!"

E. Prayer to Cleanse Your Home from Demonic Influence

"Father, I dedicate my home to You. I command every unclean spirit that has entered through past sin, cursed objects, or occult activity to leave now, in Jesus' name. I anoint this house with Your presence and declare that only the Holy Spirit is welcome here. Every assignment of the

enemy is canceled, and this place is now a dwelling of peace, righteousness, and joy!"

Scriptures for Spiritual Warfare and Victory

Use these verses when battling the enemy and to strengthen your faith in deliverance.

Authority Over the Enemy

- *"Behold, I give you the authority to trample on serpents and scorpions, and over all the power of the enemy, and nothing shall by any means hurt you." (Luke 10:19 NKJV)*
- *"Submit to God. Resist the devil, and he will flee from you." (James 4:7 NKJV)*

Power of the Blood of Jesus

- *"And they overcame him by the blood of the Lamb and by the word of their testimony." (Revelation 12:11 NKJV)*
- *"In Him we have redemption through His blood, the forgiveness of sins." (Ephesians 1:7 NKJV)*

Deliverance from Fear & Anxiety

- *"For God has not given us a spirit of fear, but of power and of love and of a sound mind." (2 Timothy 1:7 NKJV)*
- *"The Lord is my light and my salvation; whom shall I fear?" (Psalm 27:1 NKJV)*

Breaking Strongholds & Mind Renewal

- *"For the weapons of our warfare are not carnal but mighty in God for pulling down strongholds." (2 Corinthians 10:4* NKJV)
- *"Do not be conformed to this world, but be transformed by the renewing of your mind." (Romans 12:2* NKJV)

Overcoming Sin and Temptation

- *"Sin shall not have dominion over you, for you are not under law but under grace." (Romans 6:14* NKJV)
- *"I can do all things through Christ who strengthens me." (Philippians 4:13* NKJV)

Signs That Deliverance May Be Needed

If someone is showing persistent signs of demonic oppression, they may need deliverance. Here are some common indicators:

Spiritual Symptoms:

- Strong resistance to prayer, worship, or reading the Bible
- Hearing voices or intrusive thoughts that torment
- Blasphemous thoughts about God that won't stop
- Uncontrollable rage or violent behavior

Emotional & Behavioral Symptoms:

- Repeated cycles of addiction (pornography, drugs, alcohol, gambling)
- Unexplained depression, suicidal thoughts, or constant fear
- Uncontrollable sexual urges or perversion

- Sudden and irrational hatred toward Christian things

Physical Symptoms During Prayer:

- Feeling paralyzed or oppressed in sleep (sleep paralysis)
- Uncontrollable shaking, screaming, or unnatural body movements
- Feeling choked, dizzy, or unable to breathe when praying
- Eyes rolling back, growling, or unnatural resistance to deliverance

If these signs are consistently present, the person may need intentional deliverance ministry.

How to Lead Someone Through Deliverance
(Step-by-Step Guide)

If you are leading someone through deliverance, follow these steps in order:

1. Begin with Worship and Prayer

- Invite the Holy Spirit to take control of the session.
- Ask Jesus to reveal any hidden demonic influences.

2: Lead the Person in Repentance and Renunciation

- Have them confess any known sins and ask for forgiveness.
- Have them renounce any past agreements with sin, occult practices, or generational curses.

3: Command the Demons to Leave

- Speak with authority in Jesus' name: *"I command every unclean spirit to leave now! You have no right to stay. Get out in Jesus' name!"*
- If a demon resists, ask the Holy Spirit to reveal any remaining legal rights.

4: Fill the Person with the Holy Spirit

- After deliverance, have them invite the Holy Spirit to fill every empty place.
- Pray for protection and encourage them to build their spiritual life.

5: Give Them Biblical Instructions on How to Stay Free

- Read the Word of God daily.
- Pray and worship consistently.
- Surround themselves with strong believers.
- Remove all temptations and open doors.

You Are Called to Walk in Freedom!

Deliverance is not just about getting free—it's about staying free and helping others walk in victory. Keep growing, keep praying, and never stop advancing the Kingdom of God!

Are you ready to live a life of total freedom? The journey is just beginning!

ABOUT THE AUTHOR

Tom Cornell is the Senior Leader of SOZO Church in Washington state, founder of Walk in the Light International and SOZO Network. Tom is married to his beautiful wife Katy and lives in the Puget Sound area with her and their three kids. He has been in ministry pastoring and teaching the body of Christ since 2008.

He has a passion to see the body of Christ moving from people with an orphan mindset to that of sonship; equipping the body to do the work of Jesus resulting in seeing the Kingdom of God manifested here on earth.

www.ingramcontent.com/pod-product-compliance
Lightning Source LLC
LaVergne TN
LVHW052036080426
835513LV00018B/2355